A Breath of EAST ANGLIA

Bluebells and maple trees
Blickling Wood, Norfolk

Dawn breaking over the **Stour valley, Essex**

A Breath of
EAST ANGLIA

a refreshing profile of

Cambridgeshire, Essex, Norfolk and Suffolk

by **Rod Edwards**

with a foreword by Ronald Blythe

JARROLD
PUBLISHING

DEDICATION

For my close family, without whose help and support
all of this would not have been possible

ACKNOWLEDGEMENTS

Whilst there are many people who have aided me in the production
of this book, some people do deserve a special mention.

I would like to thank Antony Jarrold who gave me the
opportunity to work on this, my first book, and Mike Fuggle,
for his guidance in its design.

Thanks also to the National Trust and English Heritage,
who allowed me to photograph their properties and historic sites
and all other owners of the East Anglian properties that I have
photographed for this book.

Finally, thanks also to Fuji Films, whose vibrant, colourful and
sharp emulsions have been used exclusively in all of the
photographs in this book.

Hardback   ISBN 0-7117-1025-2

Paperback   ISBN 0-7117-1026-0

Photographs and text © Rod J. Edwards 1998

Published by Jarrold Publishing, Norwich 1998

Book design by Mike Fuggle

Printed in Great Britain by Jarrold Bookprint Ltd 1998

CONTENTS

Freezing fog in pine forest at **Brandon, Suffolk**

Blossom time, **Norwich Cathedral Close, Norfolk**

FOREWORD

BY RONALD BLYTHE

*T*HESE stunning pictures succeed in their dual purpose of bringing East Anglia to those who do not know it, and in making those who do, see it all over again, but with new eyes. This is one young traveller's vision of what to many of us is a scene made familiar to us by artists, composers and writers, and by a whole host of guides, and yet the strength of Rod Edwards' views lies in their being able to open-up this celebrated corner of Britain in such a way as to cause us to feel that we are journeying through it for the first time. Many of the photographs belong to the early morning when landscape and architecture alike possess an intensity unlike that of any other hour of the day, and such as in the misty, waking picture of Dedham Vale, and in the harsher studies of the Fens. The world has a way of being date-less at dawn, also owner-less. Everything, from glorious Ely to the Southwold bathing-huts, exists in an element which only the camera can describe. The proof of good photography lies in its being part actuality, part mystery. It should create vivid recognition and also dream. For it to be more than some automatic response to a subject, it must stand a certain scrutiny – a kind of imaginative looking into. These pictures of a much-photographed East Anglia possess this criteria and are fresh and beautiful.

Rod Edwards remembers that however inland one is there prevails a marine climate and a watery-ness, plus a cutting wind and a burning sun. He notes how so many great buildings in the area stand flat against the sky, like brilliant stage-sets, and indeed were intended to do so by those who made them. He also captures East Anglia's special solitude and, here and there, its emptiness, its scenes where human activity has given up and left behind a few artifacts to show what once happened in them. An abandoned plough, the strangely powerful litter of Shingle Street, the ruins of Burgh Castle like broken old teeth. But though often thoughtful and moody, these photographs frequently evoke the exhilaration of Suffolk and Norfolk particularly, counties which stimulate the senses still, as they did long ago when they bred a tough race of farmers, merchants and craftsmen whose achievements continue to fill us with wonder. Books like this are here to jog our complacency, to make us alert to what surrounds us, or for the visitor to what could be for him a unique journey eastwards.

RB

CAMBRIDGESHIRE *pages 14-37*

EAST ANGLIA
map showing the locations of the photographs

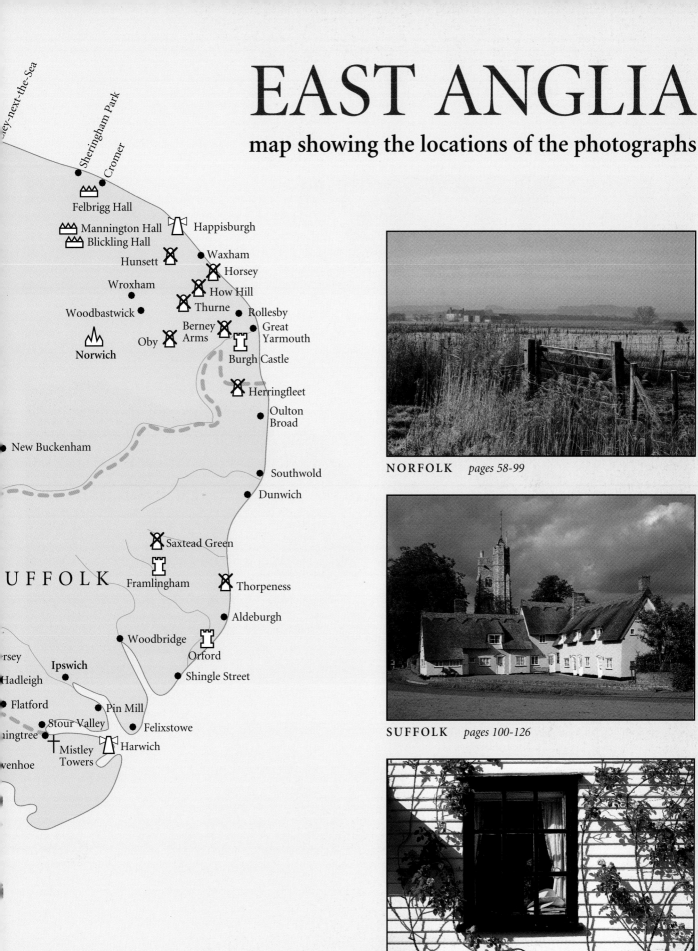

...ey-next-the-Sea
Sheringham Park
Cromer
Felbrigg Hall
Mannington Hall
Blickling Hall
Hunsett
Happisburgh
Waxham
Horsey
Wroxham
How Hill
Thurne
Woodbastwick
Rollesby
Berney
Arms
Great
Yarmouth
Oby
Norwich
Burgh Castle
Herringfleet
Oulton
Broad
New Buckenham
Southwold
Dunwich
Saxtead Green
SUFFOLK
Framlingham
Thorpeness
Aldeburgh
Woodbridge
Orford
...rsey
Ipswich
Shingle Street
Hadleigh
Flatford
Pin Mill
Stour Valley
Felixstowe
...ingtree
Mistley
Towers
Harwich
...venhoe

NORFOLK   *pages 58-99*

SUFFOLK   *pages 100-126*

ESSEX   *pages 38-57*

Dawn, **Salhouse Broad**

INTRODUCTION

*T*HERE is a special quality to East Anglia which has inspired a succession of artists, writers, and composers over many centuries. Their work has been partly stimulated by the vastness of its landscape and its low, sandy shores giving way to estuaries where the whispering of the reeds is occasionally interrupted by a scurrying moorhen or the stately rise of a heron as it leaves its fishing-place.

The region takes its name from the Angles, people who invaded England from Germany and Denmark in the fifth and sixth centuries, ending Romano-British rule and setting up their own kingdoms in middle and eastern England. East Anglia is bounded to the south by Greater London, to the west by the shires of the east Midlands, and to the north and east by the low and vulnerable coastline facing the North Sea.

Nature-lovers will find a lot to enjoy in East Anglia but so too will those who love history and architecture. Towns and villages have picturesque cottages as well as magnificent medieval churches to attract those who leave the main roads. Major tourist centres include Norwich, which has thirty-one medieval parish churches plus a wonderful cathedral and one of the finest castles to be seen anywhere. Cambridge is another city famous for its wealth of ancient buildings many of which belong to

Ely cathedral, Cambridgeshire

the colleges of the university founded in 1284. Ely's great cathedral which rises like a battleship above the level fens surrounding it is less famous than it should be and this is also true of Peterborough cathedral which has a west front crowded with stone figures and a richly painted nave ceiling.

Away from the long coastline East Anglia's scenery is much more diverse than might be expected. The fertile clay soils of Norfolk, Suffolk and Essex are devoted to arable farming, but lanes and tracks thread their way between the fields and there are still many ancient oaks which could once have featured in Constable's paintings. A spine of chalk runs south westwards through East Anglia from near Hunstanton on

Breckland tractors, Norfolk

Blood-red carrstone, Hunstanton, Norfolk

the Wash to leave the region at Ickleton close to Royston (it continues to Avebury in Wessex). This, later known as the Icknield Way, was an important route in prehistoric times when the going was easier on the chalky uplands rather than through densely wooded valleys. The chalk downland near Newmarket where south-west Suffolk merges with Cambridgeshire gives a rolling countryside reminiscent of Sussex, and its smooth grassland has supported horseracing since the seventeenth century.

The land to the south and east of Newmarket is the highest in East Anglia, much of it being 400 feet (122 metres) above sea level. In Norfolk countryside 200 feet (61 metres) above sea level is considered hilly and since there is no higher land to the east before Siberia the winter climate can be harsh. To the west of Newmarket and Cambridge are the fens which until 400 years ago was a boggy and inaccessible wilderness where the few inhabitants smoked opium to ward off the ague caused by mosquitoes and damp. Fenland extends northwards to the Lincolnshire border and the Wash, the latter a shallow estuary much less extensive today than it was in the thirteenth century when King John's treasure was lost – the packhorses carrying it became enmired and sank into its murky depths.

Fenland towns were originally crowded onto the rare islands rising a little above the miles of water and reedbed. The fens were drained by engineers from Holland in the seventeenth century and the peaty, inky-black soil, much of it below sea level, is amongst the most productive and valuable in England. The level landscape has a magic of its own, its beauty best appreciated when the days are short and the shadows long.

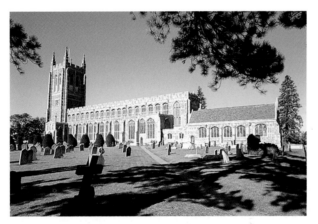

Holy Trinity church, Long Melford, Suffolk

The landscape and buildings of a region inevitably reflect its history and this is particularly true of East Anglia. Its splendid churches are the result of the prosperity generated by the wool produced in the Middle Ages by the flocks of sheep which grazed the rich pastures. Landowners spent vast sums on building and decorating these churches, employing masons and craftsmen to outdo the magnificence of churches in neighbouring parishes, possibly in the hope of reward in heaven. At about the same time they began to move out of ancestral castles into more comfortable manor houses. Tenants and peasants lived in farmhouses and cottages built haphazardly along the winding lanes between church and manor. The eccentric pattern of these rural communities usually survives today and helps give East Anglia its unique and enduring pictorial appeal.

'The Backs', Cambridge   A popular way of seeing the sights of Cambridge is by hiring a punt
on the River Cam. The river passes behind many of the colleges (hence 'The Backs' of the colleges)
and punting is a peaceful way of discovering why Cambridge University is considered to be
such a privileged seat of learning. Cambridge casts a unique spell on a late summer's afternoon
when the ancient bricks and stones are bathed in mellow light.

Cambridgeshire

*A*LTHOUGH much of the westernmost county of East Anglia lies either a little below or a little above sea level, to the south of Newmarket there are hills which almost reach the dizzy height of 400 feet (122 metres). Cambridge itself is overlooked from the south by the Gog Magog Hills whose name commemorates the last two survivors of the race of giants conquered by Brutus who, in mythology, subsequently founded Britain. The hills are their burial mounds. Cambridge is on the River Cam or Granta and grew from a Roman settlement founded in AD70. After the endowment of Peterhouse College in 1284 the town (which only became a city in the 1970s) grew rapidly as a centre of learning initially attracting many scholars from its slightly older rival, Oxford. The magnificent architectural heritage of Cambridge largely derives from the university buildings which are well seen from the flat-bottomed punts which are the most practical way of navigating the river.

The county's two other cities, Ely and Peterborough, both have magnificent cathedrals. The one at Ely dates from 1081 and originally had a central tower. However this collapsed in 1322 and was replaced by the elegant octagonal lantern which is the cathedral's most celebrated architectural feature. The eight oaken pillars which support the timber structure are each 63 feet (19 metres) long and together support a weight of 400 tons. The Lady Chapel is a further triumph of medieval engineering as when it was built it had the widest span of 46 feet (14 metres) of any vaulting in England, and its centre is only 13 inches (33 centimetres) higher than the sides.

Peterborough's cathedral is less ancient than Ely dating from the mid-twelfth century and only becoming a cathedral in 1541. Its ornate west front, featuring twin towers, pinnacles and three soaring arches, is very impressive as is the wooden ceiling of the nave which is 700 years old and richly painted. The cathedral close offers a restful oasis to visitors, as elsewhere Peterborough's character is that of a thriving modern city, its prosperity based on retailing and new technology.

Many of the lesser known treasures of the county are hidden away in its villages and small towns, and these often give a unique insight into the various influences which have moulded the history and landscape of Cambridgeshire. Visit Wisbech, for example, to appreciate the extent of Dutch influence. The 'Adventurers' from the Low Countries were the specialist engineers brought in by the Duke of Bedford in the seventeenth century to drain Fenland. They constructed the new rivers and dykes which seem to give the landscape an unworldly geometrical precision. Originally lined by windmills which pumped water from dykes into the rivers, these were replaced by steam and then electric pumps which robbed the fens of one of its most picturesque features. The old post mill at Wicken Fen is the only survivor of many thousands of drainage mills whose sails once turned and gave life to an otherwise empty landscape.

CAMBRIDGE

(1)

Trinity College (1)   A punt makes its lazy way beneath Trinity bridge. In 1546 the two colleges of Michaelhouse and King's Hall merged to form Trinity College. Sir Isaac Newton, Alfred Lord Tennyson and Lord Byron were members of Trinity, as was Prince Charles.

(2)

(3)

Queens' College and the Mathematical Bridge (2)   The bridge is based on James Essex's eighteenth century design which was made solely of pegged timbers, and used no screws or bolts. The college was founded in 1446 but was re-endowed by Margaret of Anjou, queen of Henry VI, and then by Elizabeth Woodville, child-bride of Edward VI. These two queens gave the college its name.

Clare College and bridge (3) The origins of Clare College go back to 1326 when it was founded as University Hall. Twenty years later it was re-founded by Elizabeth de Clare, the grand-daughter of Edward I. Its bridge, the oldest spanning the River Cam, was built in 1638 by Thomas Grumbold. A segment missing from one of the stone balls on top of the balustrade is said to have been a protest from the mason to the college as he was only paid three shillings for his work.

St John's College and the Bridge of Sighs (4)   Founded in 1511 by Lady Margaret Beaufort, St John's College takes its name from the Hospital of St John which had occupied the site since the thirteenth century. The picturesque Bridge of Sighs was built in 1831 to connect the older parts of the college to the new court on the opposite side of the river.

(4)

(5)

King's College Chapel and the Fellows' Building (5)   Henry VI laid the foundation stone of King's College Chapel on 25 July 1446 though work on it was not completed until the reign of Henry VII, seventy years later. This is held to be the finest Gothic building in Europe, with the breathtaking intricacy of its fan vaulting and glowing stained glass. James Gibbs' Fellows' Building flanks the chapel to the south, its simple classical design accentuating the pinnacled grandeur of its neighbour.

Punting the Cam (6)   The tower of the chapel of St John's College is seen in the background here as the river Cam meanders its way through 'The Backs'. Sir Gilbert Scott originally planned the chapel with a spire (1869), but a member of the college promised to put up £1000 a year for a tower to be built instead. Unhappily after two instalments he died in a train crash and the college had to pay the remainder.

The Senate House (7)   The Palladian building completed in 1730 is a splendid eyecatcher at the end of King's Parade. It is the venue for graduation days (called 'General Admission' here) and other ceremonial events of the university.

(6)

(7)

PETERBOROUGH

(1)

(2)

(3)

Wansford (1)   This attractive village is on the River Nene which provides the boundary between Cambridgeshire and Northamptonshire. A long stone bridge dating back to the sixteenth century takes the Great North Road over the river here, though the modern highway bypasses the village.

Peterborough cathedral (2) The cathedral was originally a Saxon Benedictine monastery founded by Peada, Christian king of Mercia in AD 655. The great west front is a fitting overture to the splendour the visitor will find inside. The current building dates from the twelfth century though 'new building' took place between 1496-1508 when fan vaulting, which compares well with that of King's College, was put up above the retrochoir. The earlier Norman work includes the original timber ceiling of the nave.

The Customs House (3)   Its name is misleading since the handsome eighteenth century riverside building has never served this purpose, being at different times a granary and warehouse. At present it is used by Sea Cadets.

CAMBRIDGESHIRE FENS

(1)

Hundred Foot Washes (1)   The strong unforgiving winds and driving rain of a fenland winter can often cause flooding. The water levels of the Old and New Bedford Rivers rise over the banks and spill into the Hundred Foot Washes. These act as an overflow area between the parallel courses of the rivers and save the surrounding fenland from flooding.

Each winter the whole area is attractive to wildfowl and three reserves have been established – two at Welches Dam near Manea and another at Welney.

(2)

Vermuyden's Drain (2)   Also known as Forty Foot Drain, this is the straight drainage dyke that cuts through the fens from near Ramsey to link up with the smaller Sixteen Foot Drain and the Old Bedford River to the east. The Dutch drainage engineer Cornelius Vermuyden, with the help of his fellow 'Adventurers' and the finances of the Earl of Bedford, transformed the marshy waterlands of Cambridgeshire during the mid-seventeenth century. He divided the Great Level into the three parts which survive today – the North, Middle and South Levels. Each Level was cut by a network of drains which eventually flowed into the Wash via sluices like the one at nearby Denver.

(3)

Fen drain, Horseway (3) Winter is a dramatic time of year to visit the fens on days when the air is crisp and the skies clear as crystal. Then the low light plays on the landscape like lights on a stage. The fringes of reeds adorning the dykes are turned golden and contrast strikingly with the dark wintry waters beyond.

Fen near Upwell (4)   An old rusting plough stands forlornly by the dark fen edge. Having served its days it is now just a reminder of the agricultural heritage of the fens.

(4)

Wicken Fen (5)   This is the last part of fenland to remain undrained and is also the oldest nature reserve in England. Purchased by the National Trust in 1899 is is unique for its enormous variety of insect and plant life, including the recently rediscovered Fen Violet. The wooden windpump is a rare survivor of many hundreds which once adorned the landscape of the fens and broads.

Wimblington Fen (6)   The wide skies are a feature of the fens and were perhaps best described by Charles Kingsley in his novel *Hereward the Wake*: 'Overhead the arch of Heaven spread more ample than elsewhere, as over the open sea; and that vastness gave, and still gives such cloudlands, such sunrises, such sunsets as can be seen nowhere else within these isles'.

Canary Cottage, Thorney (7) This quaint cottage, unusual even in fenland, stands alone in the open fields under the 'arch of Heaven'. It is privately owned and not open to the public but its charm can be admired from the road between Guyhirn and Thorney.

(5)

(6)

(7)

ELY

The river at Ely (1) The River Great Ouse pursues a slow and tortuous course between Huntingdon and Ely, with the great cathedral – 'the ship of the fens' – in the distance for much of the way. The marina at Ely provides moorings for pleasure craft which now dominate a river formerly busy with commercial traffic, much of it to the local Maltings which now serves as a multi-purpose hall.

Oliver Cromwell's House (2) Formerly the vicarage of St Mary's church at Ely, this house overlooking Palace Green was where Oliver Cromwell lived with his family between 1636 and 1647.

Ely cathedral (3) In 673 St Etheldreda, queen of Northumbria, founded a religious community on the Isle of Ely, which in those days was surrounded by marshland penetrable only by river. Over the following centuries the settlement at Ely suffered many setbacks but nevertheless grew to become a successful monastery. In 1081 Abbot Simeon began the work which was to transform a humble abbey church into a spectacular masterpiece of Romanesque architecture. The wooden Octagon, built to replace the original central tower which collapsed in 1322, is a feature unique to Ely. The medieval buildings of King's School cluster around the cathedral and incorporate some of the walls of the original monastery.

(1)

(2)

(3)

THE RIVER NENE

(1)

St Wendreda's church, March (1)
In previous centuries the spire and tower of St Wendreda's must have been a welcome landmark for travellers making for March through the flat and otherwise featureless fenland. The dedication to St Wendreda is unique – she was the sister of St Etheldreda who founded the monastery at Ely. The church has a splendid double hammerbeam roof with 118 winged angels carved to give spiritual as well as physical support.

(2)

The North Brink, Wisbech (2)
The North Brink faces the River Nene and is lined by houses which Pevsner considered to make it 'one of the most perfect Georgian streets in England'. Wisbech remains a busy market town and its industries reflect its position at the heart of a region famous for its fruit and vegetables.

(3)

Peckover House, Wisbech (3)
Owned by the National Trust, Peckover House provides an important example of eighteenth century domestic architecture. The Peckovers were a Quaker family who founded a bank which merged with Barclays in 1896. The last member of the family, the Hon. Alexandrina, gave the house to the Trust in 1943.

THE RIVER GREAT OUSE

(1)

The Turf Maze, Hilton (1)
The maze is unusual in having a monument at its centre – to William Sparrow who created it in 1660 possibly to celebrate the restoration of King Charles. However there may well have been a maze here before that and even the present one has been re-cut seven times. Local legend has it that young men walked the maze to see whether they would be lucky in marriage. If they stumbled or took a wrong turning the match would prove disastrous, or they could choose to sign a pact with the Devil if this seemed an easier way out. Mazes were also supposed to have been designed to thwart the Devil who could only travel in a straight line.

The Marina, St Neots (3)
The Marina is actually sited to the south of St Neots close to the village of Eaton Socon where the River Ouse flows northwards through a succession of verdant meadows.

St Neots (2)   The town was once a busy staging-post on the Great North Road but the modern road bypasses the town though some of the old coaching inns survive. St Neots takes its name from an obscure Celtic saint whose remains were enshrined in a Benedictine monastery established here in the tenth century. Having been sacked by the Vikings the priory and the saint's bones were moved to the Abbey of Bec in Normandy in 1081.

Oliver Cromwell's statue, St Ives (4)   Oliver Cromwell was born in Huntingdon, lived for a time at Ely, and farmed at St Ives where his statue overlooks the market-place. After the execution of Charles I in 1648 Cromwell became Lord Protector and governed England until his death in 1658.

(2)

(3)

(4)

OLD HUNTINGDONSHIRE

(1)

Houghton Watermill (1) The weatherboarded watermill is a famous beauty-spot on the Great Ouse between Huntingdon and St Ives and is owned by the National Trust. There has been a watermill on this spot for over one thousand years and flour is still produced here on the regular milling days.

Hemingford Grey (2) With its neighbour, Hemingford Abbots, the village is sited on the Great Ouse downstream from Huntingdon. It owes its beauty to the riverbank trees and the delightful church, its spire truncated by a freak hurricane in 1741.

(2)

Huntingdon (3) This was a county town before the old shire of Huntingdon was swallowed by Cambridgeshire. It is linked to Godmanchester by a fourteenth century bridge over the River Ouse and is famous for having been the birthplace of Oliver Cromwell in 1599 and the home of the poet William Cowper in the eighteenth century.

(3)

ANGLESEY ABBEY

Anglesey Abbey (1)   The landscaped gardens that surround Anglesey Abbey are amongst the finest in England. An Augustinian priory was founded here by Henry I in the twelfth century which lasted as a monastery until 1535 when it was dissolved by Henry VIII. The buildings were subsequently incorporated into an Elizabethan manor which has been owned by Thomas Hobson of 'Hobson's Choice' fame, Sir George Downing who gave his name and a substantial endowment to Downing College, and the American-born Lord Fairhaven. The Abbey is owned by the National Trust and the magnificent Fairhaven collection of paintings and furniture is on show to visitors.

(1)

The Temple Lawn (2)   This part of the garden at Anglesey Abbey was laid out in 1953 to celebrate the coronation of Queen Elizabeth II. Ten Corinthian columns of Portland stone are surrounded by an oval hedge and the entrance is guarded by lead figures of a lion and lioness. At its centre is a marble statue by G. Fossi, 1801, which is a copy of Bernini's masterpiece, David. Anglesey Abbey is in the village of Lode, six miles north east of Cambridge.

(2)

(3)

The Hyacinth Garden (3)   At the heart of this formal garden is the
statue of Old Father Time inspecting a sundial. Although the garden
takes its name from its display of hyacinths in springtime, the beds are
colourful throughout the months when Anglesey Abbey is open.

White weatherboarding This type of facing is characteristic of Essex and is particularly common in waterfront towns like Burnham-on-Crouch and Maldon. White weatherboard gives old houses and cottages a sparkling appearance which contrasts well with the weathered brick of neighbouring buildings.

Essex

*T*HE untidy sprawl of Greater London marks the southern boundary of both Essex and East Anglia. To the east the county has à flat shoreline indented by several wide estuaries which provide the home of countless yacht clubs. The resorts of Clacton and Southend-on-Sea are less popular with holidaymakers than they used to be but both still provide all of the amenities demanded by today's day trippers.

To the north, the River Stour provides the boundary with Suffolk and the valley which features so often in the paintings of John Constable. The beauty of villages such as Dedham and Stratford St Mary beguiles the visitor today in much the same way as it attracted Constable whose father was a local miller.

Essex has borders with Hertfordshire and Cambridgeshire to the west and this side of the county also has its share of picturesque villages and appealing old towns. The old way of life of rural Essex may be diluted in places like Saffron Walden or Thaxted where many of the inhabitants commute to London or Cambridge, but the ancient churches and cottages are painstakingly maintained and are as beautiful today as at any time in their long history.

Colchester is the pick of the larger towns of the county and its Roman name (Camulodunum) is the first record of a British town to appear in written history. Soon after its foundation by the Romans it was sacked by Queen Boudicca, but after her subsequent defeat Camulodunum was rebuilt and fortified by the Romans. Colchester castle, now a museum, is remarkable both for the Roman masonry which survives in its walls and for its exhibits which shed light on the long and often violent history of the town.

The estuaries of the rivers Crouch, Blackwater, Colne and Stour, each with their maze of narrow creeks extending far into lonely marshes, were ideal for smuggling in the old days when brandy and tobacco were illicitly imported. Two hundred years ago many of the delightful weatherboarded pubs here would have played an important role in these activities, just as further inland village pubs could well have been the headquarters of 'the gentlemen of the road'. Dick Turpin, England's most celebrated highwayman, was born in the Rose and Crown at Hempstead (then named the Bell Inn), but seldom plied his trade in Essex. Like most of his kind, his career ended on the gallows. Some village pubs have mementos which reflect forgotten customs. Curious discs with nails hammered through their centres surround a window of the Cross Keys at White Notley, a village on the road between Braintree and Maldon. They commemorate the days when waggoners used to stay at the inn overnight. Any newcomer to the trade stopping at the Cross Keys for the first time had to buy a round of drinks and pin a coin to the wall with a nail from the village blacksmith. Some of the coins have been there for 250 years or more.

Wendens Ambo This attractive row of thatched and plastered cottages leads to a lovely church which is unusual in having a short spire, reminiscent of the 'Hertfordshire spike', surmounting the tower. The small village is situated about two miles south west of Saffron Walden. The unusual and rather lovely name of Wendens Ambo is derived from Wenden (winding stream) and the Latin *Ambo*, meaning 'both', signifying that in 1662 Great and Little Wenden were joined together to make one village.

COLCHESTER & RIVER COLNE

(1)

The Keep, Colchester Castle (1)
This was the largest keep ever built by the Normans (work on it was carried out between 1076 and 1125) which occupies the site of the vast Temple of Claudius erected here by the Romans a thousand or so years before. The lack of good native building stone led the Normans to re-use Roman building material. The stone foundations of the temple were particularly useful. The castle is now a museum with fascinating exhibits tracing the long and eventful history of the town.

Oysters (3)   The Colne estuary and salt water creeks surrounding Mersea Island have been famous for their oyster beds since Roman times. To celebrate this Colchester holds an Oyster Feast each October when the mayor invites guests to sample the first fruits of the new oyster season at a banquet in the Town Hall.

(2)

(3)

Wivenhoe (2)　Two miles south of Colchester, Wivenhoe's narrow streets are lined with old houses and lead down to a waterfront which has changed little in two hundred years. This has been a shipbuilding centre since the reign of Elizabeth I and work on small boats continues today, the smell of woodvarnish tingeing the soft sea air. On 22 April 1884 the village suffered from an earthquake which damaged more than two hundred buildings but there is little to disturb the peace of Wivenhoe today except the creaking of old damp ropes chafing against wooden hulls and the slap of rigging against masts.

THAXTED

(1)

The Almshouses and John Webb's Windmill (1) These lovely cottages with pretty gardens and latticed windows are hidden away on the edge of the churchyard at Thaxted. John Webb's windmill, built in 1804 by the local farmer who gave his name to it, overlooks the town. There is a fine view of the town and surrounding countryside from the top of its tower if you are energetic enough to climb the wooden ladders.

(2)

Thaxted Guildhall (2)   This delightful fifteenth century building is one of the most-photographed in East Anglia, especially as its neighbours are equally as appealing. Thaxted's prosperity came from two industries in medieval times, beginning with cutlery which was later overtaken by the cloth trade. The church is large and airy and dates from the mid-fourteenth century though there were constant additions to its fabric and furnishings throughout medieval times as the townspeople became increasingly wealthy. It is claimed that Dick Turpin once worked in a butcher's shop which is now a cottage adjacent to the Guildhall.

Clarence House (3)   This elegant building stands opposite Thaxted church. Built in 1718 of red brick to a square plan it is an excellent example of a town house built in the time of Queen Anne and Sir Christopher Wren, its formal design is perfectly at ease with the more haphazard styles of nearby cottages.

(3)

TURPIN TERRITORY

(1)

Saffron Walden (1)   The town takes its name from the saffrons (better known to us as crocusses) which were grown here through the centuries when the East Anglian wool trade was flourishing. Saffron was an important dye used in finishing the cloth and in Tudor times a visitor described Saffron Walden as a 'town surrounded by fields smiling with pleasant saffron'. Set amidst the rolling hills of north Essex, it remains a town with charisma today, even though it has lost its acres of yellow crocusses. It has St Mary's church with its soaring spire, the ruins of a Norman castle, a remarkable earth maze, and streets of old houses and inns, some of them colour-washed and pargeted. Pargeting is the name given to moulded plasterwork specially popular in the eastern counties and an excellent example is to be seen on the walls of the Old Sun Inn, now a books and antiques shop. Its most famous panel shows Tom Hickathrift of Wisbech holding a wheel and axle-tree from his wagon. With the former as a shield and the latter as a weapon he was able to defeat the formidable giant which is shown facing him.

(2)

Townsford Mill, Halstead (2)
This attractive watermill with white weatherboarding so typical of Essex stands over the River Colne beside a row of weavers' cottages. Originally built as a corn-mill, it was adapted by Samuel Courtauld for the manufacture of silk during the early nineteenth century but is now used as a warehouse for antique furniture.

Finchingfield (3)   The pond and green are at the heart of this village and make a scene which has always been a favourite with artists and photographers. The church tower, topped by an unusual eighteenth century cupola, can just be seen above the red-tiled roofs of the cottages, while from the opposite direction the picturesque postmill is a natural eyecatcher in the distance. No doubt Dick Turpin, the notorious 'gentleman of the road', frequented some of the several public houses that can be found in the village.

(3)

THE STOUR ESTUARY

(1)

(2)

The Low Lighthouse, Harwich

(1)   This unusual building was a favourite subject with John Constable when it served its original purpose. It is now a maritime museum with an exhibit illustrating the town's history as a port . Other attractions at Harwich include the Electric Palace cinema, the Redoubt (a circular fort built in 1808 against the threat of invasion by Napoleon), and a treadmill crane once worked by naval ratings as a punishment in bygone days.

Harwich (2)   Rich in maritime history and heritage, the town of Harwich is all too easily ignored by those who merely visit Parkeston Quay for the departure of their ferry. In the past Harwich has had strong links with famous seamen like Raleigh, Drake, Frobisher and Nelson. A lesser-known name amongst them is that of Christopher Jones, the Master of the *Mayflower*, who sailed with the Pilgrim Fathers on their voyage to America.

(3)

Mistley (3)   In the eighteenth century Richard Rigby of Mistley Hall tried unsuccessfully to develop Mistley as a spa town. He also commissioned Robert Adam to build a new church which met with disapproval from the parishioners. In Victorian times they demolished the nave and built another church closer to the village, fortunately leaving the two classical towers which had once stood at each end of Adam's church. Nowadays Mistley flourishes as a port, trading timber and grain.

Manningtree (4) In the Middle Ages the River Stour was navigable upstream to Sudbury and Manningtree was a flourishing seaport. Since then the river has become silted and the small town lost its trade to Ipswich and Harwich so that perhaps it was inevitable for Manningtree to become Britain's smallest market town. Manningtree was the home of Matthew Hopkins the infamous 'Witch-Finder General' who in 1645 earned prodigious sums and a wretched reputation in his search for unfortunates accused of witchcraft in East Anglia.

(4)

ESSEX CASTLES
AND A SAXON CHURCH

(1)

(2)

(3)

The Castle Keep, Castle Hedingham (1)   This impressive Norman stronghold stands on a wooded knoll overlooking the River Colne and the village which takes its name. Aubrey de Vere, earl of Oxford, built the castle in 1140 and his descendants own it today. The keep is 100 feet (30 metres) high, has two corner turrets and contains a banqueting hall with a minstrels' gallery. The original drawbridge over the moat was replaced by an elegant brick bridge in 1500 which would have been crossed by Henry VIII and Queen Elizabeth I when they visited Hedingham Castle.

The Castle, Hadleigh (2) Hadleigh Castle was built in 1232 by Hubert de Burgh, earl of Kent and once one of the most important men in the kingdom. The ruins are on a commanding site overlooking the Leigh marshes and the Thames estuary and have long been a source of inspiration for artists, amongst them John Constable who painted a sombre impression of them in 1828, following the death of his wife Maria.

St Andrew's church, Greensted (3)   The walls of this church still have split oak logs put there by its builders in 845 when it was founded. Its appearance has changed a lot since then, but the dormer windows and weatherboarded tower give it a unique charm. It is peacefully situated next to a farmyard about a mile from Chipping Ongar.

ESSEX COASTLINE

Burnham-on-Crouch (1)
Regarded by many as the Cowes of the east coast, this attractive little place has far more to offer than the appeal of its waterfront. The elegant red brick Georgian houses lining the High Street are punctuated by pretty weatherboarded cottages and there is an unusual Victorian clock tower. In late summer every year yachts of all shapes and sizes participate in the seven days of racing known as Burnham Week – a must for the keen yachtsman's diary.

(1)

Tollesbury (2)   The main industry at Tollesbury, oyster fishing, has declined and the little town is now a quiet place where one can savour the solitude of the surrounding saltmarsh and enjoy fresh sea breezes. These sailmakers' lofts at Woodrolfe Creek, a short distance from the town, are unusually well preserved. High tides flood the road which passes them and submerge the bottoms of the ladders which give access to their upper floors.

(2)

(3)

Hythe Quay, Maldon (3)   The ancient fishing port is situated at the point where the River Chelmer joins the head of the Blackwater estuary. From the town centre back streets lead down to Hythe Quay where warehouses, ship-chandlers, and boathouses line the waterside. Thames barges are amongst the interesting variety of boats which may be seen here.

LAYER MARNEY TOWER

Layer Marney Tower The great six-storey gatehouse, built in 1520 of red brick, was intended to be the entrance to a mansion of equal grandeur. It was built by Lord Henry Marney who died three years later with only the the west wing finished. On the death of his only son in 1525 the Marney family became extinct. From the top of the tower, visitors can see wonderful views to the Blackwater estuary and beyond. The adjacent church has the Marney family tombs with their colourful effigies and a late medieval wallpainting of St Christopher.

Burnham Norton   One of six 'Burnhams', Burnham Norton is scattered with wooden farm buildings and old flint houses bearing quaint but apt names like 'Sea Peeps' and 'Creek Cottage'. The village is reached by way of a quiet, twisting lane which leads off the north Norfolk coast road to head for the flat Norton marshes. The beauty of the landscape is well seen on a cold December morning, when copper-coloured reeds wear a coat of rime frost.

Norfolk

ORFOLK is the most maritime of the East Anglian counties with a coastline which faces east, north and west. Much of its shore is low with sand dunes giving scant protection to low lying land behind it when tides are high and the winds onshore. For a brief space where the coast turns southwards to face the Wash there are cliffs 50 to 60 feet (17 to 21 metres) high, with bands of chalk above blood-red carrstone. However at each end of this outcrop the contours drop and the usual character of the shoreline is restored. Inland the landscape is largely given to agriculture, with the small fields of yesteryear gathered into vast expanses which grow crops of barley, wheat and rape. Where lighter soils prevail, in the Breckland of south and west Norfolk, there are extensive tracts of forest. The original heathland of the area is preserved and is used as a Battle Training Area by the army.

The Norfolk Broads owe their existence to peat diggings which became flooded by the adjacent rivers, the slow-flowing Bure, Ant and Yare. Before the coming of railways these waterways were vital to the transport system of the area and were plied by a fleet of wherries in all seasons, but now they have two faces – busy with holidaymakers in the summer in their luxurious hirecraft, deserted in the winter when the landscape recaptures its timeless beauty and romance.

The county's unofficial motto is 'Du Different' (note that even the spelling follows this maxim) and this is true of many aspects of Norfolk throughout its history. It has been claimed that it is the rigours of the county's winter climate that breeds larger-than-life characters, some of them heroes, a few villains. One of the former was Horatio Nelson who was born in Norfolk at Burnham Thorpe in 1758 and joined the navy at the age of twelve to rise to become England's most successful admiral (reflected in the number of pubs in Norfolk called 'The Hero' which bear his portrait on their signs). After victories over the French at Cape St Vincent and the Battle of the Nile (1798), Nelson was mortally injured at Trafalgar in 1805, with his death in the arms of Captain Hardy in his hour of triumph being one of the most poignant scenes of British history.

Thomas Coke of Holkham, earl of Leicester, had a less spectacular life but his innovative ideas concerning the crop rotation and other principles of agriculture meant that England was able to produce home-grown food cheaply in order to sustain the early generations of industrial workers. Coke's estate at Holkham is centred on a mansion built by William Kent which is one of the county's showpieces. Sandringham, H.M. the Queen's Norfolk home, is situated nearby. Edward, Prince of Wales bought the estate in 1861 despite Queen Victoria's disapproval, and ever since this has been a favourite home with a succession of monarchs. Holkham and Sandringham are both open to the public in the summer and so are other historic houses in the county, notably Blickling, Houghton, Oxburgh and Felbrigg.

NORWICH

(1)

Norwich Cathedral (1)   Work started on building the cathedral in 1096. The epic proportions of this undertaking can only be appreciated with the knowledge that all of its facing stone was imported from Caen in Normandy. The spire topped by a gilt finial is 315 feet (96 metres) high and is a famous feature of the cathedral, though visitors will probably find the elaborate vaulting of the nave with its 225 coloured roof bosses equally memorable. The abundance of windows and the light colour of the Caen stone gives the interior an airy spaciousness which makes Norwich cathedral unique and reflects similar qualities to be found in many of East Anglia's parish churches.

Elm Hill (3)   Norwich compares favourably with other cities more celebrated for their medieval character, and certainly its thirty-one surviving medieval churches are unmatched elsewhere. Similarly Elm Hill has few rivals as a medieval street with its array of lovely old houses facing each other across the narrow cobbled thoroughfare.

(2)

(3)

Pull's Ferry (2)   The picturesque Norwich building is a fifteenth century watergate which had a ferryman's house and inn attached to it. It took its name from John Pull, a formidable character who was ferryman and landlord in the nineteenth century. The Normans built a canal to the cathedral in order to bring stone from Normandy to the building site and the watergate protected this access to the city. The canal was filled in *c.*1780 and the roadway which follows its former course is now part of the cathedral close.

KING'S LYNN

(1)

(2)

(3)

(4)

The Waterfront (1)   King's Lynn was at the height of its prosperity in medieval times when it was at the centre of the trade exporting to the continent, woollen cloth woven in East Anglia. Its two market places, one holding a market on Tuesdays, the other on Saturdays, are both overlooked by magnificent churches.

The fishing fleet (2)   Lynn (as it is known by locals) is situated close to the mouth of the Great Ouse, which when the tide drops lives up to its name by oozing its lazy way through the mudbanks facing the waterfront. Fishermen sail out into the Wash for their catches of shrimps, cockles and mussels from this inlet just north of the town centre.

The Guildhall and Old Gaol House (3)   The Guildhall was built in 1421 by the Guild of Holy Trinity, an influential body of Lynn merchants. Its flint façade has a distinctive chequer pattern and a fine Perpendicular window. The brick-built Old Gaol House is next door, its purpose declared by the carving of a set of manacles above the entrance. It is now a museum charting the history of crime and punishment through the centuries.

The Custom House (4)   This elegant little building on Purfleet Quay dates from 1683 when it was built by Henry Bell, the architect responsible for several other attractive buildings in the town. It has recently been renovated and is now used as the Tourist Information Centre.

WEST NORFOLK

(1)

Hilgay Fen (1)   To the south and west of King's Lynn the level fens seem to go on to infinity. Hilgay village is on the main road between Ely and King's Lynn but its fen is in lonely countryside to the west. Here the fields are covered by hoar frost giving the landscape the flavour of a fairytale world.

(2)

(3)

Great Massingham (2) This village lies to the east of King's Lynn close to the Peddars' Way, the pre-Roman road which strikes southwards across the length of East Anglia. Great Massingham has a large duckpond at its centre and its waters reflect the tower of the church and the huddle of houses and cottages which surround it.

Castle Acre Priory (3) Castle Acre village is almost entirely contained within the area of the great castle erected here by William de Warenne, the Conqueror's son-in-law, to protect the place where the Peddars' Way crosses the River Nar. With their castle completed, the de Warennes set about building a monastery for the Cluniac order and this became a place of pilgrimage when it acquired the arm of St Philip, a relic famous for its properties of healing. The Prior's Lodging is the only part of the monastery to survive intact, though the magnificent west front of its church also stands as a monument to the monks who worshipped here through the centuries.

(4)

Sandringham House (4)   H.M. the Queen's private Norfolk home, Sandringham has belonged to royalty since 1862, when Queen Victoria reluctantly agreed to buying the estate as the private residence of the Prince of Wales. In 1870 the Prince pulled down all of the existing house except the conservatory and built a much larger new one in Jacobean style. This remains the heart of the present house though there have subsequently been many additions and alterations. Sixty acres of gardens, parkland and lakes surround the house which is open to the public in the summer when it is not used by the Royal Family.

Caley Mill, Heacham (6)   If you like the smell of lavender then nowhere in England is more fragrant than Caley Mill in midsummer. Fields of different lavenders surround the nineteenth century mill and the miller's cottage next to it, which are the centrepiece of Norfolk Lavender, a tourist attraction which is also a successful industry.

(5)

Hunstanton (5)   The resort is situated at the point where the Norfolk coastline turns to face the waters of the Wash and is thus the only place on the east coast where the sun sets over the sea. At the north end of the shore, cliffs striped with layers of blood-red and gingerbread carrstone are a striking contrast with the sandy beaches to the south.

(6)

NORFOLK COASTLINE

(1)

Cley Mill (1)   Although officially known as 'Cley-next-the-Sea', the sea is a mile away from the village, though it has a nasty habit of making a return if there are onshore winds and a tidal surge. The windmill is world-famous, having featured in so many paintings and photographs, and dates from the early eighteenth century. Strangers to the district should know that Cley is pronounced 'Cly', another example of Norfolk's individuality.

(2)

Cromer (2)   In *Emma,* Jane Austen wrote of Cromer as 'the best of all sea bathing places', but it was not until the coming of the railways to the town that it became truly popular as a seaside resort. Cromer remains a favourite place with holiday-makers today, and they enjoy the heathland nearby as well as its cliffs and sandy beach. The Cromer fishermen launch their boats from the beach to catch crabs which are celebrated throughout the land for their size and flavour.

Sheringham Park (3) The National Trust own the landscaped parkland surrounding Sheringham Hall in north Norfolk. The park was landscaped by Humphrey Repton who began his work in 1812. It became his favourite project and today's visitors see it in its maturity with plantings of rhododendrons and azaleas, a colourful bonus in spring and early summer. This temple is at one of the park's viewpoints – there are others where specially-built towers take viewers above the trees to see stunning views of the coastline and countryside.

(3)

Thornham (4)   Situated between Hunstanton and Brancaster on the north Norfolk coast road, Thornham village was once closer to the sea and able to support its own fleet of fishing boats. Today the letting of holiday cottages is an important money-earner for local people, and many of the boats pulled up above the tideline look sadly abandoned.

Thornham Creek (5)   This village marks the western-most point of the north Norfolk coastline, an area which is particularly popular with ornithologists.
Shellfish are a delicacy on this coast and whelks and winkles could be on the menu at any of the excellent pubs and restaurants in the neighbourhood of Thornham. Samphire is another delicacy to be found on the salt marshes here and its tangy, fleshy leaves are pickled to make a healthy and appetising starter or snack.

(4)

(5)

(6)

Brancaster Staithe (6)   There
was a Roman garrison at
Brancaster in the early years of
the first millennium and it is
easy to sympathise with its
members who must have longed
for home as they looked out over
the salty wastes from their
outpost of empire. Yet today
many people come to this part of
the coast to enjoy the qualities
which were so alien to the
soldiers of long ago.

(8)

(7)

Brancaster Staithe (7)   East Anglian sunsets are specially spectacular near the coast where the sky makes such an important contribution to the scene. Brancaster Staithe is the home port for many Norfolk yachtsmen, though they have to be very conscious of the state of the tide before arranging arrivals or departures.

Fishermen at Brancaster Staithe (8)   The mudflats and sands of this coastline support a wide variety of shellfish. Cockles, mussels, whelks and winkles are all prized, though the industry supports far fewer fishermen than it did in the past. Many have converted their boats so that they can take visitors to view the seabirds and seals on Scolt Head Island.

Burnham Overy Staithe (9)
There are six villages bearing the prefix 'Burnham', ranging in size from the large village of Burnham Market to the tiny hamlet of Burnham Overy close by. The little River Burn reaches the sea at Burnham Overy Staithe which is in effect a separate village, some way from Burnham Overy itself. Boats ferry bird-watchers from the staithe to Scolt Head Island, an RSPB sanctuary.

Burnham Thorpe (10 and 11)
Horatio Nelson was born in this village in 1758 where his father was the parson. He was baptised in tiny All Saints' church, a place of pilgrimage for admirers of the great admiral who lived in the village from 1787 until 1793. The church was restored in his memory and contains many naval mementoes including the white ensign flown by the Second World War battleship, HMS *Nelson* and also a bust of Horatio Nelson.

(9)

(11)

(10)

(12)

Burnham Overy watermill (12)
The picturesque mill dates from
the eighteenth century and used
the waters of the River Burn
which seldom seem to flow fast
enough nowadays to be able to
power a waterwheel. In its heyday
the mill would have been a busy
place, with farmers bringing
wagon-loads of corn meeting
here and, no doubt, discussing
the appalling weather and
iniquitous price they were being
paid by the miller.

(13)

Wells-next-the-Sea (13)   The small coastal port of Wells-next-the-Sea remains a busy trading town and a popular destination for holidaymakers. The quay actually lies a mile from open water, the result of the construction of a sea-wall in the nineteenth century, which enabled land to be reclaimed from the coastline. A channel through the sea-wall now provides access to the quay for the local trading vessels. The town itself is characterised by quaint cottages and narrow streets called 'yards'. Visitors to Wells-next-the-Sea can reach the sandy north-facing beach on foot, by road or by miniature railway.

Blakeney (14)   Still, clear days are rare on the north Norfolk coast but provide magical landscapes when they occur.

(14)

Blakeney (15)   Like most of the small harbours on the north Norfolk coast, Blakeney's quays and river were once busy with commerce whereas today they belong to yachtsmen and pleasure boat-owners.
On a warm summer evening, it's a pleasure to saunter along the waterfront, watching boats catching sea breezes and little children fishing for crabs with a hook and line.

Morston (16)   This is a lovely backwater coastal village which becomes busy in early summer when bird-watchers migrate here to take boat trips to Blakeney Point. This is a National Trust property, a sand and shingle spit 3½ miles long where many rare seabirds nest, amongst them terns, oyster catchers and ringed plovers. In winter large flocks of brent geese feed on the neighbouring marshes.

(15)

(16)

(17)

Little Walsingham (17)   In 1061
the lady of the manor, Richeldis
de Faverches, was at prayer when
she had a vision of the Virgin
Mary who took her to Nazareth
to show her the childhood home
of Jesus. When the same vision
was repeated twice more
Richeldis became convinced
that it meant that she should
build a replica of the house at
Walsingham, and this she did.
It subsequently became a shrine,
an important place of pilgrimage
which at one time rivalled that of
the shrine of St Thomas à Becket,
and the tradition continues to
this day with many thousands of
devout pilgrims visiting the
village each year. The medieval
priory at Walsingham became
one of the richest in England
though little remains of it today.
The bricks of the sixteenth
century conduit house at the
centre of Little Walsingham must
have heard much gossip and
scandal in the days before
running water came to the
village.

(18)

Great Yarmouth (18)   Today Yarmouth is the premier resort town of the east coast but it had a comparatively late start as a holiday resort, only developing in the latter part of the nineteenth century. Before this it depended on its traditional industry, herring fishing. However the 'silver darlings' deserted this part of the North Sea after the Second World War and Yarmouth then turned to other industries (notably servicing the offshore gas field). Yarmouth's heritage as a seaport is reflected in the buildings along the riverfront and occasionally by a visiting ship. Here a replica of Captain Cook's HMS *Endeavour* is moored next to the preserved steam drifter *Lydia Eva* opposite the Town Hall on South Quay.

Waxham (20)   The coastline north of Great Yarmouth has low sand-dunes held together by tough marram grass to resist strong onshore winds. Nevertheless the shore is retreating inland and occasionally the inroads made by the sea are disastrous to man and beast.

(19)

Happisburgh (19)   The striped tower of the lighthouse situated on low cliffs just north of Great Yarmouth has been a landmark since 1791. However it did little to help the HMS *Invincible* which struck the offshore sandbank and went down with all 119 hands in 1801 while en route to join Nelson's fleet blockading Copenhagen. Note that the name of the village is pronounced 'Hays-burra'.

(20)

NORFOLK BROADS

(1)

(2)

Hunsett windmill (1)   The windmill was built to lift the waters from the dykes draining the Broadland marshes into the River Ant. It is one of the best-known beauty spots on the Norfolk Broads. Both the mill and its gardens are private.

Thurne Dyke windpump (2) The white-painted mill is of a different design to the one at Hunsett but was built to serve the same purpose. At the height of the holiday season Thurne Dyke becomes crowded with hire craft. Lovers of the Broads may try to avoid the waterways in high season, preferring to see them in early summer or autumn when the rivers are virtually deserted except for the wildlife.

(3)

Oby windmill (3)   The third windmill stands on the banks of the River Bure, one of many lining the course of the river between Great Yarmouth and Wroxham. Oby's name shows that the village is of Danish origin, like many others in Broadland. Slowly but inexorably many of these romantic ruins are sadly crumbling away through the passing of time and the action of the elements.

(4)

Wroxham (4) Out of season the dykes and riverbanks are full of hire boats waiting for their first letting. These dayboats are at Wroxham, the 'capital of the Broads', where the River Bure flows beneath a seventeenth century bridge at the centre of the village – a bottleneck that can cause the occasional delay to traffic.

(5)

(6)

Woodbastwick (5)   The village green at Woodbastwick, with its thatched cottages and church, is one of the pictorial gems of Broadland. The dedication of the thatched church of St Fabian and St Sebastian, is believed to be unique in England. The village is also famous for having a brewery which regularly wins national awards for the excellence of its real ales. The village sign shows a man tying up his leggings with wood bast (flexible fibrous bark of trees), hence the name Woodbastwick.

Rollesby Broad (6)   The road between Acle and Caister-on-Sea passes through 'a Trinity' of beautiful broads which are cut off from the Broadland rivers. Rollesby is the largest of the three, the others being Ormesby and Filby. The Broads were not created by Nature but are the results of ancient, man-made peat diggings which then became flooded early in the Middle Ages.

(7)

Horsey windpump (7)   Horsey dyke takes the navigable waters of the Broads to within a mile of the North Sea. The drainage mill stands at the head of the dyke and is owned by the National Trust which also cares for Horsey Mere, one of the loveliest expanses of water in Broadland. The Trust have made footpaths around the edge of the mere which give opportunities to spot some of the shy species of birds living in marshland.

Burgh Castle (9)   Although standing only a few feet above sea level, the ruins of Burgh Castle provide a wonderful viewpoint over southern Broadland. The Romans built their stronghold here in the late third century to guard against Saxon raiders. Like Berney Mill it is cared for by English Heritage.

(8)

(9)

Berney Arms Windmill (8)
The seven-storey mill is one of the grandest landmarks of the Broads and can be seen from many miles away. It stands on the banks of the River Yare close to where it flows into Breydon Water and is most accessible by boat. However the more adventurous may like to undertake the long walk across the marshes from Halvergate or Great Yarmouth or take one of the rare trains scheduled to stop at Berney Arms station. The mill belongs to English Heritage and is open to visitors in the summer.

The Reed Cutter, How Hill (10)
Norfolk reed has the reputation of being the 'prince' of all thatching materials, easily outlasting straw. Eric Edwards has been a marshman for the Broads Authority for over thirty years and each winter harvests the reed beds. Dressed in a blue smock with thigh-length waders and a well-worn worsted hat, he cuts through layers of reed with a scythe and ties them into bundles ready for market. Whilst much of the reed is now harvested with a mechanical cutter, Eric occasionally likes to revert back to the more traditional methods of reed cutting.

(10)

BRECKLAND

(1)

Thetford Forest (1)   More than eighty square miles of forest cover Breckland, most of it monotonous plantings of Corsican and Scots pines. However some trees native to Breckland survive, like these venerable beeches at Two Mile Bottom near Thetford.

(2)

East Wretham Heath (2)
The Devil's Nightcap' is the name given locally to the early-morning mist hanging over the mere at East Wretham Heath. There is a small area here where the indigenous vegetation of Breckland is preserved and visitors can see the heathland plants, birches and Scots pines which covered the district before forest and prairie-style agriculture took over.

Masonic Hall, Thetford (3)
The Hall was a watermill in a previous existence when it was known as the Old Pit Mill. It stands on the bank of the River Thet which originally provided power for its waterwheel. Although adopted as a London overspill town in the 1950s, Thetford still has several fine buildings which illustrate the history of the town. There are the remains of a Norman castle and Cluniac Priory, an Ancient House which has its original timber framing and dates from the fifteenth century, and the Bell Hotel which was once a famous coaching inn and has the persistent (but tolerated) ghost of an ostler.

(3)

(4)

Worthing (4)   Barley is a traditional crop with Norfolk farmers and is used by brewers and distillers, and for animal feed. A second agricultural revolution has transformed parts of Norfolk into prairies, and trees and hedges have vanished as fields have been enlarged to accommodate ever bigger and faster machinery. These endless acres are at Worthing in the heart of Breckland.

The Buckenhams (6)   Old Buckenham is spread around a wide green and has byways with intriguing names like Cake Street, Hog's Snout, Puddle Dock and Hoos Wroo, each sounding like a magical place from a child's storybook.
New Buckenham (pictured) has an older feel, and it was here in the twelfth century that William d'Albini built an earthen mound and topped it with a circular keep that is supposed to be the earliest example in England. The Court House built in 1559 stands at the centre of the village, the room standing on pillars. The one in the middle served as a whipping post for miscreants and its iron manacles are still attached. The attractive row of cottages shown here is delightfully typical of the village.

(5)

(6)

Wayland Wood, Watton (5)
The wood is known locally as 'Wailing Wood' and used to cover a far greater area than it does today. It was large enough in bygone times to give us the legend of the Babes in the Wood, though it seems harmless enough in Spring when the ground is carpeted with bluebells. The wood is to be found two miles south of the sleepy market town of Watton.

GREAT HALLS AND GARDENS

(1)

Blickling Hall (1)   This magnificent Jacobean mansion stands on the site of a moated medieval manor house which belonged to the Fastolf (Shakespeare's Falstaff) and then the Boleyn families (legend has it that Anne was born at Blickling). In the early seventeenth century the estate came into the hands of Sir Henry Hobart who engaged Robert Lyminge as architect for his new house which was built between 1616 and 1627. Today Blickling and its lands belong to the National Trust with meticulously maintained gardens being surrounded by acres of mature parkland, the latter criss-crossed by footpaths. Inside, the house has beautifully furnished staterooms with outstanding tapestries. There was considerable redecoration in Georgian times but the Long Gallery, with its extravagantly carved plaster ceiling, remains unaltered.

The Gardens (2 and 3)   In the front, the hall is flanked by yew hedges which are almost as old as the house. At the back there are extensive formal gardens which were laid out for the Marchioness of Lothian in 1872 and then remodelled in the 1930s by Mrs Norah Lindsay. She replaced some of the innumerable small beds with broad gravel paths and greensward and left the distinctive yew topiary and curved hedges. Beyond the garden the parkland contains a crescent-shaped lake more than a mile long, a Temple with a secret garden close by, a remarkable mausoleum in the shape of a pyramid, a look-out tower and, closer to the house, an elegant Orangery built *c.*1820 to the design of John Repton, Humphrey Repton's son.

(2)

(3)

Felbrigg Hall (4)   This is another fine Jacobean house in the care of the National Trust. The house was built for Thomas Wyndham in 1620 but was enlarged 1674-87 and again in the mid-eighteenth century. The Wyndhams were a family who loved art and scholarship, and the paintings at Felbrigg together with the books in the library reflect their wide interests. William Wyndham collected paintings, china and furniture for the house when he took his Grand Tour of Europe as a young man in the eighteenth century.

Felbrigg Hall gardens (5)   The octagonal dovecote is a feature of the walled garden and once housed two thousand white doves. The garden has recently been restored as a 'Potager' – a decorative kitchen garden with herbs, fruit trees and fragrant flowers. There are also walks through the lovely park to the ancient church (with its monuments of the Felbrigge [sic] and Wyndham families), to the lake, and to the Great Wood which has a nature trail.

(4)

(5)

(6)

Mannington Hall (6)   If you look at any large scale map of Norfolk a major feature are the numbers of moats that are marked. These show the sites of medieval manor houses, and most of these vanished long ago. However the one at Mannington survives and surrounds a picturesque flint house dating from 1460. Visitors to Mannington in summer will enjoy its famous rose gardens and the nature trails which take them to interesting parts of the estate.

(7)

Oxburgh Hall (7)   A further example of a moated manor house can be found in west Norfolk where Breckland merges with the fens. Oxburgh Hall was built in 1482 by the Bedingfeld family and their descendants still live there even though the hall and estate were bequested to the National Trust in 1952. The outstanding feature of the building is the 80 feet (28 metres) high gatehouse, made of locally fired bricks which originally faced anyone coming over the drawbridge (the latter was replaced by a bridge in 1710). From the time of the Tudors until the restoration of Charles II the Bedingfelds suffered from being Catholics in a county which was almost entirely Protestant. Oxburgh was sacked and burnt during the Civil War when Sir Henry Bedingfeld was captured by Cromwell after the battle of Marston Moor in 1644. The family's fortunes subsequently improved and the house was enlarged in 1775 by Sir Richard Bedingfeld who pulled down the medieval Great Hall on the south side of the house (one of the finest in England) and built a Saloon to house his paintings.

(8)

The Parterre (8) The formal beds of the parterre with their rounded box trees were modelled on a design from Versailles and were laid out in the 1840s soon after the chapel had been added to the house by Pugin. In summer when it is planted with silver, yellow and blue bedding plants it is an attractive feature of the gardens at Oxburgh.

Cavendish   The group of pink-washed thatched cottages in front of St Mary's church makes a famous scene
that captures the very essence of Suffolk. The Dukes of Devonshire take their family name from the village –
in the Middle Ages the family derived much of their wealth from the district.

Suffolk

SUFFOLK is the most easterly county in England, its coastline extending from Lowestoft in the north to Felixstowe in the south. At Lowestoft the fishing industry remains but is far less important than in its heyday earlier this century. At that time steam drifters were moored five-deep at the quays and women travelled south from Scotland in special trains to gut the herrings and pack them into salt-filled barrels. The sandy coast here remains popular with holiday makers and the sea is faced by a succession of caravan parks and holiday camps.

Felixstowe, which also has a share of the holiday trade, is more famous as a busy ferry and container port fed by the important cross-country A14 road. The smaller coastal resorts of Southwold and Aldeburgh have shunned the attractions which made Yarmouth, Clacton and (to a lesser extent) Lowestoft popular and both places take their air of exclusivity into the twenty-first century. Aldeburgh is famous for having been the home of Benjamin Britten whose opera *Peter Grimes* brilliantly captures the spirit and character of this part of the world.

The county is unusual in having no city within its boundaries but to compensate for this it has a fine selection of market towns and a host of lovely villages. Bury St Edmunds has a cathedral and many other beautiful buildings while Ipswich, the county town, is a place where modern architecture dominates the handful of houses which survive from earlier centuries. The magnificence of Suffolk's parish churches is legendary with those at Blythburgh and Long Melford being particularly famous, their size and elaborate decoration deriving from profit from the wool trade in medieval times. Unfortunately these days many of the more isolated churches are locked, but it is well worth seeking out the keys to be able to see lesser-known treasures from the county's great architectural heritage.

Suffolk also has its share of castles and stately homes. Amongst the latter Ickworth is outstanding, being built by Frederick Hervey, 4th earl of Bristol and Bishop of Derry in 1792. The building is vast, with two blocks in classical style (each one a mansion in itself and intended to house the earl-bishop's collection of statues and paintings) linked to a magnificent central rotunda. Gardens and a landscaped park surround the buildings and all of it is in the care of the National Trust.

Framlingham Castle is the most impressive of Suffolk's castles because of its size and location – it faces a wide, reed-fringed lake. Dating from the early years of the twelfth century, it had a chequered history and at different times was eventually used as a prison and poorhouse. Like Framlingham, Orford Castle is an English Heritage property. The stronghold once covered a considerable area overlooking the lonely marshes but now only the cylindrical keep remains. Dating from 1165 and standing 90 feet (27.5 metres) high with walls 10 feet (3 metres) thick, it would have had to have been a brave commander who decided to storm its elaborate defences.

IPSWICH

(1)

The Wet Dock, Ipswich (1)   In 1845 lock gates were built so that the port of Ipswich retained its waters as the tide fell. At this time the Wet Dock was the largest in Europe and must have been picturesque with square-rigged barques moored next to smaller Thames barges with their ochre-coloured sails. The Old Customs House is a handsome building in Palladian style built the year before the Wet Dock opened. The docklands at Ipswich have been rejuvenated with many old warehouses converted into modern offices and the area is now fashionable with a range of pubs and restaurants.

(2)

The Ancient House (2)   Also known as Sparrowe's House after the wealthy merchant who once lived here, the beautiful building dates from 1567. Its front is decorated with pargeted figures illustrating four continents – Australia is absent as it still awaited discovery. Some of the plasterwork figures are slightly bizarre, like the semi-naked man with feather head-dress who represents America.

Pin Mill (3)   The mill which gave this popular boating place on the River Orwell its name produced the wooden pegs which were once vital for pinning the planks and beams of vessels together. It was this tidal haven that inspired Arthur Ransome to write *Swallows and Amazons.* The Butt and Oyster public house which was first licenced in 1553 stands by the water's edge and was one of his favourite haunts.

(3)

NEWMARKET

(1)

(2)

Newmarket (1)   The Jubilee clocktower stands at the crossroads in Newmarket where the Norwich to Cambridge road crosses the one from Ely to Bury. Fortunately the town is now bypassed as traffic used to face interminable delays here.

Newmarket's history as a horse-racing centre began in 1605 when James I, an ardent man of the turf, found that the springy grass covering firm, chalky soil gave superb conditions for racing.

(3)

The Jockey Club and National Horseracing Museum (3) The bronze figure of the most famous racehorse of all, Hyperion, stands outside the Jockey Club in the High Street. The museum stands next to the Jockey Club and occupies the former Regency Subscription Rooms. It opened in 1983 and has a wide variety of exhibits illustrating Newmarket's four hundred years of racing history.

The Gallops (2) Stable lads have to rise before dawn to take the first strings of horses for their morning exercise. The activity carries on until mid-morning with groups of riders making their way on to the Gallops on Newmarket Heath so that their form at full speed can be assessed by the stable's trainer. Newmarket has two racecourses, the Rowley Mile Course where the Guineas meetings are held and the July course whose atmosphere is less formal.

BURY ST EDMUNDS

(1)

The Abbey Gardens and cathedral (1) Bury St Edmunds manages to be a cathedral town without being a city. Its cathedral was originally a sixteenth century parish church dedicated to St James, but this was adopted as a cathedral in 1914 and greatly enlarged in the 1960s and 1970s with work continuing to the present day. Like the great abbey in whose grounds it stands, the cathedral is dedicated to St Edmund, king and martyr, who was killed by the Danes in 869.

The abbey held relics of St Edmund and became a great centre of pilgrimage. Two of its gates, one Norman, the other medieval, survive intact, but little else remains standing, though the crumbling walls are impressive in showing the size of the monastery in its heyday.

(2)

(3)

Angel Hill and Abbey Gate Street (2)   The rectangular street plan of Bury St Edmunds derives from that drawn by Abbot Baldwin at the time of the Norman Conquest. The town is proud of its buildings which are of a wide variety of styles and periods, and few other towns can have so many Georgian shopfronts. The Angel Hotel gives its name to Angel Hill and remains as picturesque today as it was in Dickens' time when he used it as a location for one of the episodes in *The Pickwick Papers*.

Ickworth House (3)   Frederick Hervey, 4th earl of Bristol and Bishop of Derry built Ickworth House in 1792. He was an immensely wealthy nobleman who had a passion for building large houses and for collecting paintings and sculpture. Ickworth was built to accommodate his collection. He intended to live in the oval-shaped central rotunda while his paintings and statuary were to be displayed in the pavilions at either end of the curving wings. Ickworth is a treasure-house again today with paintings by Titian, Gainsborough and Velasquez and a matchless collection of Georgian silver. It is a National Trust property.

SUFFOLK WINDMILLS

(1)

Thorpeness postmill (1) The mill dates from 1803 and was moved to its present position from neighbouring Aldringham in the 1920s. Thorpeness is a village created at the beginning of the twentieth century as a sort of rural version of a garden city. The houses are grouped about a large lake and nearly all of them are in half-timbered, mock Tudor style. 'The House in the Clouds' is the most spectacular of these – it is a water-tower converted into a house. The postmill stands close by.

(2)

Herringfleet windpump (2) The little mill was built in 1820 to help drain the reedy marshes on the Suffolk side of the River Waveney. It soon became redundant as steam and then electric pumps were introduced to lift water from dyke to river. Most of the windpumps which lined Broadland rivers have become derelict but the one at Herringfleet is fortunate in being preserved.

Saxtead Green Post Mill (3) With a post mill the whole structure turns on a great timber post to face the wind, the fan tail providing the power to do this. A mill was recorded on this site as early as 1309, but the present mill was built in 1796 and continued to work until 1947. It is preserved with all of its machinery intact by English Heritage.

(3)

CONSTABLE COUNTRY

(1)

(2)

(3)

Willy Lott's Cottage (1)   The Vale of Dedham, where the River Stour meanders amongst the meadows seen in the paintings of John Constable, belongs to both Suffolk and Essex. The cottage appears in Constable's most famous work, *The Hay Wain* and the scene has changed little since the time the artist originally painted his canvas. Willy Lott was its tenant at the time and he worked for the miller at Flatford Mill on the other side of the millpond.

Flatford Mill (2)   The mill is owned by the National Trust but is leased out to serve as a field study centre and so is not generally open to the public. It is situated at the heart of the Constable Country and features in one of the artist's finest works *(Flatford Mill from a Lock on the Stour)*. Constable spent much of his boyhood at the mill where his father was the miller and it is scenes such as this that in his own words 'made me a painter'.

Dedham (3)   The village of Dedham (actually in Essex) is at the heart of the Constable Country. The artist went to the grammar school here and attended St Mary's church whose tower often appears in his landscapes. The village was the birthplace and home of a later East Anglian artist, Sir Alfred Munnings, who was also skilled in capturing the essence of the region in his work.

SUFFOLK COASTLINE

(1)

Dunwich (1)   Looking at this stretch of pebble beach it is difficult to imagine Dunwich as one of the most prosperous ports in England but in the early years of the fourteenth century it was a town with several churches, two monasteries and about five thousand inhabitants. However, in January 1326 the sea broke through the primitive sea defences and piled up a great bank of shingle to move the mouth of the River Blyth northwards. The harbour at Dunwich disappeared and relentless erosion over subsequent centuries has seen the town disappear beneath the waves. Now there is only the leper chapel standing next to the nineteenth century parish church to remind us of the former glories of Dunwich.

(2)

Aldeburgh (2) The town was a busy port in the Middle Ages when cloth was exported to Flanders and the Low Countries. The half-timbered Moot Hall, built *c*.1512, is a reminder of the town's dependence on trade in the past. Today Aldeburgh is a seaside town loved by those who do not mind its pebbly beach or lack of the sort of tourist attractions to be found at Great Yarmouth or Clacton. Its unique qualities attracted the great composer Benjamin Britten to the town, and he founded the summer music festival which brings music-lovers to the town each June for concerts in Snape Maltings and at churches in the neighbourhood. Britten's greatest opera, *Peter Grimes*, is based on narrative verse by George Crabbe who was born in the town in 1754.

(3)

The House in the Clouds (3) Thorpeness was created as a holiday village before the First World War by the writer Glencairn Stuart Ogilvie. The houses he built are in a pot pourri of styles ranging from Tudor semi-mansions to rustic Suffolk cottages with tar-painted weatherboarding. Remarkably their façades conceal their concrete construction. The House in the Clouds, which stands close to the postmill, was also built by Ogilvie and was originally a water-tower. The mill was moved here from Aldringham in the 1920s and was used to pump water into the tank concealed at the top. The tower is now a converted house.

(4)

Shingle Street (4)   The Suffolk
coast inspired M R James to
write ghost stories which are
unsurpassed for their atmospheric
settings and sense of foreboding.
These haunting qualities may
well be felt at lonely places like
Shingle Street at the southern
end of Orford Beach, where only
the echoing sounds of gulls keep
you company.

(5)

Felixstowe (5)   The container port has seen fantastic growth in the last thirty years and is now one of the busiest in Europe. The northern side of the town, away from the mouth of the River Orwell, has a different face and retains much of the character of a pre-war seaside resort with beach-huts and promenade.

Woodbridge (6)   The beautiful tide mill dominates the quayside at Woodbridge which these days is almost completely given over to yachts and other pleasure craft. A mill was first recorded here as early as 1170, but the present building dates from 1793 and worked until 1957. It draws its power from seawater which flows from a reservoir above the mill, filled by the previously rising tide. The railway line separates the quay from the town itself which has more than its share of lovely old houses as well as a magnificent parish church.

(6)

SOUTHWOLD

(1)

Southwold (1)   The genteel atmosphere of the resort is typified by the immaculate, brightly-painted row of beach-huts lining the promenade. The town is delightfully laid out around seven 'Greens', created after fire destroyed the town in 1659. These are overlooked by grand houses built subsequently as Southwold became fashionable. Its streets are an attractive montage of pantiled, flint and brick buildings clustering around the fifteenth century church of St Edmund, and a tall Victorian lighthouse. There are also streets of more humble dwellings where the fisherfolk used to live though today they are more likely to be holiday homes.

(2)

The Quayside (2)   The River Blyth reaches the sea just to the south of Southwold and so the harbour is situated a mile or so distant from the town itself. Boats are moored to high, rickety jetties, and fishermen take their catches to equally tumbledown huts on the riverside where they sell the fish directly to the public.

'Southwold Jack' (3)   The parish church at Southwold is outstanding even in a county of magnificent churches and has an early sixteenth century choir screen painted in glowing colours and this wooden figure of a man at arms of about the same date. He strikes a bell when a cord is pulled to announce the start of a service or the entrance of the bride at a wedding. 'Southwold Jack' is also the trademark of Adnams brewery whose beer is world-famous. The Sole Bay inn is the closest pub to the brewery and that is where the old enamel poster [shown here] can be seen.

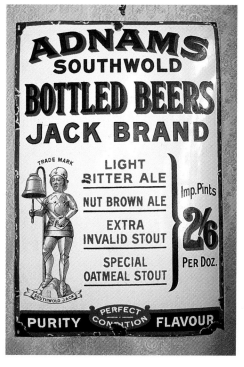

(3)

SUFFOLK WOOL TOWNS

(1)

(2)

(3)

Hadleigh – St Mary's church and Deanery Gate (1) Suffolk's Hadleigh should not be confused with the town of the same name in Essex. The lead-covered spire of St Mary's church is distinctive and sits on top of a tower which is older than the rest of the church. The imposing red-brick gateway overlooking the church-yard is all that remains of the great palace built by Archdeacon Pykenham for himself in 1495.

The Guildhall, Hadleigh (2) The beautiful Guildhall backs on to the churchyard and faces the market place at Hadleigh. The three-storied building dates from the fifteenth century and has served many different purposes through its long history having once been a school, then an almshouse and finally the town hall. Today visitors are shown the intricate crown-post roof, the Georgian assembly room, and the ballroom added to the building in Victorian times.

The Moot Hall, Sudbury (3) The timber-framed Moot Hall is of fifteenth century date and was built to be the meeting-place of the townsfolk. Sudbury was an important wool town and had three churches in medieval times as well as some fine merchants' houses. Many of these survive, and stand amongst the handsome early Georgian houses of the same style and date as Gainsborough's birthplace. The latter is now a museum and gallery which contains examples of the artist's work.

SUFFOLK WOOL VILLAGES

(2)

(1)

(3)

Kersey (1)   The village gave its name to a type of ribbed cloth popular in medieval times for being warm and hard-wearing. The ford in the middle of the village is its celebrated feature which has long been popular with artists and photographers. It is a triumph to capture the scene without unsightly cars. In bygone days the ford also served as a cart wash, a practice which might be frowned upon today.

Lavenham (2)   The innumerable colour-washed, half timbered houses of Lavenham justifiably make it the most famous of the small Suffolk towns whose fortunes were founded on the wool trade in the Middle Ages. Lavenham should not be explored without visiting the outstanding 'Wool' church dedicated to St Peter and St Paul which was largely funded by a successful local clothier, Thomas Spring. The church is large, light and airy and, unexpectedly since this was never a monastic institution, there are delightful misericords illustrating various facets of medieval life.

The Guildhall (3)   Lavenham's timber-framed Guildhall was built for the Guild of Corpus Christi in 1529 and one of its corner posts bears a portrait of the founder of the Guild, the fifteenth Lord de Vere. The nine rooms of the Guildhall, which belongs to the National Trust, have displays illustrating local history with emphasis on the development of the wool trade.

(4)

The Ancient House, Clare (4)
This charming priest's house
occupies a corner of the
churchyard at Clare, a village full
of history and beauty five miles
east of Haverhill. Known as The
Ancient House, the building
bears the date 1473 and is
pargeted (decorated with carved
plaster) with vines and other
foliage on its north face.

(5)

Clare (5)   Some say that the pretty village gets its name from the clear water of the infant River Stour though it could equally well derive from the clarity of the light. There are remains of a Norman motte at the centre of the village and a climb to the top gives extensive views over the red-tiled roofs of the cottages to the countryside beyond.

Long Melford (6)   The main street running through the parish is three miles long and this gives the village its name. The church is at the northern end of the street and provides a fitting climax since it is usually considered to be the finest in Suffolk and was even described by Pevsner as 'one of the most moving parish churches in England'. It is 150 feet (46 metres) long and was almost completely rebuilt in the fifteenth century, thus having a harmony of design which is rare in East Anglia. Melford Hall faces the church on the upper side of the broad green. It is a turreted Tudor mansion dating from 1578 and is a National Trust property.

(6)

SUFFOLK CASTLES

(1)

(2)

Orford Castle (1)   The ingenious design of the castle with multi-angled exterior walls gave a wide field of fire for the archers defending it. It was built by Henry II in 1165 with two purposes in mind – to establish the authority of the Crown in the formerly lawless district and to guard the coast against invasion. A legend from the thirteenth century tells how the castle became the home of a 'merman'. This wild old man with his bald head and long grey beard became entangled in the nets of fishermen who took him to the castle. After a few months he managed to escape back to the sea and was never seen again.

Framlingham Castle (2)   The appearance of the castle today, seen in the classic view with the lake in the foreground, is practically the same as it would have been 1213 when King John was entertained at the newly-built stronghold by its builder, Roger Bigod, second earl of Norfolk. The curtain walls link thirteen high towers, a design which crusaders brought home from the Middle East, abandoning the Norman practice of having an impregnable keep at the heart of the defences. The castle belonged to many powerful barons in medieval and Tudor times before falling into decay in the seventeenth century. After that it was used as a poor house and school and the great hall and domestic apartments became derelict. The castle is now in the care of English Heritage.

Oulton Broad　The River Waveney flows through Oulton Broad to reach the sea at Lowestoft. It is the most southerly of the broads and is always busy in the summer with hire craft and private pleasure boats. George Borrow used to live in a large house overlooking Oulton Broad which had a waterside summerhouse where he wrote *Lavengro, Romany Rye,* and other books popular with Victorian readers.

THE STORY OF
THE PHOTOGRAPHS

*A*T the age of nine, I was fortunate enough to be given my first camera by my parents. It was a very basic, disposable model with a fixed plastic lens, a hole to look through and an intriguing little red button that clicked as I pressed it. I knew nothing of the aesthetics, nor of the science of photography, but I knew that I liked pressing that little red button! And so began my love of photography.

The photographs in this book are a collection of images that have taken many months to compile. With each exposure lasting for only a fraction of a second, it seems unbelievable that the total exposure time for all of these images was no more than thirty seconds. The brief moment of exposure is the culmination of a great deal of thought and planning without which my photographs would not exist.

Whilst I spend much of my time travelling around the UK and Europe, photographing beautiful and dramatic scenery, I nevertheless hold a special affection for East Anglia. Its soft, sometimes almost shadowless light, with the absence of hills or mountains, allows me to photograph the low lying landscapes very early or late in the day, when the light is at its warmest and most photogenic. It is this quality of light, together with East Anglia's wide and sometimes dramatic skies that has challenged so many artists in the past and never fails to inspire me.

Photographing the natural landscape using available light can sometimes be frustrating and time consuming. When I visit a location for the first time, I like to familiarise myself with the place, to develop an understanding of it. I then decide upon the time of day, the season and consider the weather conditions which might be most suitable. Although the notoriously changeable British weather is a most elusive element for which to plan, quite often it is just this unpredictable element that will enable me to capture the true spirit of a place. From the frosty hayrolls in the Norfolk fens, to the vibrant sun-bathed beach huts in Suffolk, or the haunting, foggy atmosphere of Layer Marney Tower in Essex, the weather played a crucial role in each photograph.

I used a number of different cameras for the photographs in this book. They range from a portable Nikon 35mm SLR, to a Mamiya medium format camera which delivers larger transparencies and offers a significant increase in quality. Recently I have acquired a beautiful five by four inch field camera, which provides exceptional quality. It is similar in appearance to the tripod-mounted, wooden cameras used during the late nineteenth century, in the very infancy of photography. Working with its rosewood body, creaking leather bellows and squeaky brass knobs, it gives a tremendous, almost spiritual satisfaction, a feeling of being back to the very rudiments of photography.

I hope that this book will also provide for you some of the immense pleasure that I had in working on it.

Rod J Edwards 1998

INDEX